92
Nam
5-69-50

W9-AUE-609

JOE NAMATH, SUPERSTAR

by Robert B. Jackson

illustrated with photographs

Henry Z. Walck, Incorporated   New York

Lincoln School Library

The pictures on pages 7, 14, 18, 22, 26, 28, 31, 34, 35, 41, 43, 45 and 47 were supplied by Wide World Photos, Inc. Those on pages 9, 11, 19 and 37 are from United Press International.

Copyright © 1968 by Robert B. Jackson
All rights reserved. Library of
Congress Catalog Card Number: 68-23887

Printed in the United States of America

CONTENTS

1
JET UPSET

THE JETS broke from the huddle and quickly trotted to their positions. Standing behind his center, Joe Namath took a last look at the tough Boston Patriot defense. Then he crouched to set himself for the snap and began to shout signals.

Suddenly the ball was in his hands, and the two lines were colliding with bone-jarring impact. Pads thudded and players grunted as Boston linebackers as well as linemen charged at him. A Patriot "blitz" was on.

Without turning, Joe quickly dropped back into the passing pocket formed by the blocking of his teammates. He cocked his arm as he retreated, and before the onrushing Boston defense could reach him—almost, it seemed, before he had time to extend his arm or even set his feet to throw—the ball was rifling far downfield.

It was a bright and sunny Saturday in mid-December of 1966, and nearly sixty thousand football fans had come out to Shea Stadium on Long Island to see the New York Jets and Boston Patriots of the American Football League play the last game of the regular schedule for both teams.

The Jets wanted a victory over Boston that afternoon to give them a .500 season of six wins, six losses and two ties. In the early fall they had won four of their first five games and tied the other, temporarily leading the Eastern Division and raising hopes among their fans for a possible championship. But as the season continued, the Jets had slumped badly, largely because of illness and injuries to key players. They won only one game of their next eight.

Boston was concluding a much more success-ful season. The Patriots were leading the Eastern Division with a record of eight wins, three losses and two ties. They needed only to defeat the under-dog Jets to win the division title and next play

JOE NAMATH, $427,000 SUPERSTAR.

the Kansas City Chiefs of the Western Division
for the league championship.

The AFL champion would then go to Los
Angeles on January 15 for the first of the Super
Bowl meetings between the American and National
League champions. Because the Super Bowl was

being called "the biggest football game ever" by many sports experts, and since the winning players were expected to receive $15,000 each, the Boston team had much at stake that warm December Saturday.

But the New Yorkers were playing their best game of the season. The running attack, unsuccessful earlier in the year, was finally clicking, and quarterback Namath was passing extremely well. In the third quarter, New York led the favored Pats by a surprising score of 24–13.

When Boston had the ball, first and ten, on the Jet twenty-nine-yard line, it still seemed anyone's ballgame. The Patriot touchdown and extra point which seemed likely would put Boston within four points of New York.

A stout Jet defense held the Patriots to no gain on their first two downs, and on third down came the play which proved to be the turning point of the game. Babe Parilli, the veteran Pat quarterback threw hard and well, but his intended receiver ran in the opposite direction from which Babe expected. An alert Jet cornerback intercepted, New York gained control of the ball, and the Boston threat was ended.

Three plays later lanky Joe Namath was once

IN SPITE OF A HARD-CHARGING DEFENSIVE END, JOE GETS HIS
PASS AWAY AGAINST BOSTON, DECEMBER, 1966.

again skipping backwards, his shoulders hunched
characteristically forward and his white shoes
glistening in the mild winter sunlight. (Most other
players wear black shoes.) Despite the thundering

Patriot blitz, Namath threw quickly and accurately to Jet end George Sauer, Jr., who had gotten well behind his defensive man. Sauer went all the way to complete a seventy-seven-yard touchdown play; and instead of New York 24, Boston 20, the score had suddenly become New York 30, Boston 13.

The Patriots never recovered from this quick reversal of fortune, and the Jets went on to win the game 38 to 28, spoiling Boston's championship possibilities. (The next day the Buffalo Bills had an easy game against the Denver Broncos to take the divisional championship.)

The entire Jet team had shown a fine effort against one of the toughest teams in the league, but Namath had been brilliant in the best game thus far of his young career. He had completed fourteen of twenty-one passes for a total of 287 yards gained, and three of the passes had been for touchdowns.

As the happy Jet fans made their way from the stadium in the deepening twilight, Joe stayed behind on the field for a television interview. Tired and aching, he was finally heading for the dressing room when he saw a group of two dozen boys still remaining in the stands above the runway. They cheered and applauded as he trotted under

HIS KNEES HURTING BADLY, JOE WEARILY LEAVES THE FIELD AFTER THROWING THREE TOUCHDOWN PASSES AGAINST THE PATRIOTS—HIS BEST PERFORMANCE OF 1966.

them. Without looking up, he tossed the important game ball into their midst and jogged wearily from sight.

2
YOUNG JOE

JOE NAMATH was born (May 31, 1943) and grew up in Beaver Falls, a small and smoky Pennsylvania city about thirty miles northwest of Pittsburgh, near the Ohio border. Beaver Falls, located in an area rich in coal and natural gas, is primarily a mill town, with a large steel industry as well as several chinaware and cork-product factories.

The plates from which United States currency is printed are also made there, but the Namaths weren't seeing much money in those days. Joe had three older brothers and an older sister, and Joe's father, who had come from Hungary when he was a boy, worked at a furnace in a steel mill.

Although the Namath family lived in the Lower End, one of the poorest sections of Beaver Falls, Joe recalls his old neighborhood with some fondness. "It was just great, growing up there," he once told a reporter. He remembers swimming in the river, playing around the nearby bottling plant and junkyard, and hitting so many baseballs through the windows of the laundry in back of his house they were eventually boarded up.

Not far away was a metal dump where the neighborhood gangs often staged rock fights to get to the top of "Tin Hill." The rocks came from the roadbed of nearby railroad tracks. "Man, we had everything there," Joe says.

Most of the other boys living in the Lower End were Negro, and Joe has said that his first encounter with racial prejudice came when he was ten and a white woman refused to sell a pizza to him and his best friend from across the street. His strong interracial background—as a high-school senior he was the only white starter on the basketball team, for example—caused problems when he later attended the University of Alabama, but eventually proved an advantage to him in the integrated world of professional sport.

When Joe was in the sixth grade, his parents

BEFORE THE 1965 ORANGE BOWL GAME, JOE AND HIS MOTHER CELEBRATED CHRISTMAS IN A MIAMI BEACH HOTEL—FAR DIFFERENT SURROUNDINGS THAN THEY HAD KNOWN IN EARLIER YEARS IN BEAVER FALLS.

were divorced and his father moved away. There was even less cash in the house from then on, and Joe was pretty much on his own after school. He worked at a variety of odd jobs to help himself and the family. Some, like shining shoes and caddying at the golf course, were typical for small boys everywhere. Others reflected the dingy poverty of the bars and pool halls of the Lower End, and a national sports magazine has reported that Joe ran messages for men who took illegal bets on horse races.

It was a tough, gritty and highly competitive world for young Joe Namath. During his early high-school days, the possibility of going to college hardly occurred to him, seeming to be financially out of the question. He planned to join the Air Force when he graduated. Yet by the time he was finishing his senior year, over fifty colleges were offering him scholarships. The reason was football.

Joe had been a natural athlete of unusual ability ever since he was a small boy. His older brothers, Franklin and Bobby (Franklin later went to the University of Kentucky for two years on a football scholarship), taught him to play football when he was only five, although there was a family rule that he was too small to be tackled then. Before long he could throw the ball higher than the telephone wires and hit a stump forty yards away.

At six, Joe began playing Little League baseball. He soon took up basketball as well, mounting a backboard and basket on the end of a long two-by-four which he tied to the post of a street light for night games. He remembers playing basketball on the street in weather so cold he wore mittens and earmuffs, but not going down into the cellar—where he could only practice dribbling—until it actually snowed.

A star on three teams at Beaver Falls High School, Joe was the football quarterback, a guard on the basketball team, and a power-hitting center-fielder. He might easily have become a professional baseball player instead of a pro quarterback, for he was scouted in high school by half a dozen major league teams. The Chicago Cubs were especially interested in him then, and the Baltimore Orioles were still trying to sign him even after he had left Beaver Falls. But Joe's favorite sport was football, and given the chance, he wanted to go to college.

Joe had completed eighty-four of one hundred and twenty passes during his senior year at Beaver Falls High (quite modestly, he gives most of the credit to the team's excellent blocking). Also, he was playing in a region known for the high level and fierceness of its football competition. Soon offers of athletic scholarships were coming in from colleges all over the country.

Joe eventually settled upon the University of Maryland as his first choice, but he failed to meet the university's college board requirements. The coaching staff at Maryland wanted him to try the examination again, but by then he had become interested in Penn State instead.

Since Maryland played Penn State, and the Maryland coaches did not want to compete against a quarterback as good as Joe for three years, they discouraged him from going there. They phoned Paul "Bear" Bryant, athletic director and head football coach at the University of Alabama. Alabama was not only one of the major collegiate football powers, it was also not on Maryland's schedule.

An Alabama coach flew up to Beaver Falls during the summer of 1961 to bring Joe down for a look at the university, and he enrolled in the school of education shortly afterward. He soon impressed Bryant, one of the most knowledgeable and successful football coaches in the country, as "not only the best athlete I've ever coached, but the best athlete I've ever seen." Joe played first-string quarterback on an otherwise senior team his sophomore year; he completed seventy-six of one hundred and forty-six passes for 1,192 yards and twelve touchdowns. Alabama lost but one game that season.

During Joe's three years at quarterback, the Crimson Tide won twenty-nine games and lost only four. Alabama went to a major bowl game at the end of each of his three seasons as well, defeating Oklahoma in the Orange Bowl in 1963 and Missis-

COACH BEAR BRYANT WORKS WITH JOE DURING AN ALABAMA PRACTICE SESSION.

sippi in the Sugar Bowl in 1964, then narrowly losing to Texas in the Orange Bowl of 1965.

Joe found the life of a varsity athlete at a big-time sports school much to his liking. He lived with the rest of the football team in Paul W. Bryant Hall, a super-plush dormitory for athletes, sometimes called the "Bear Bryant Hilton" by students and a far cry from the drab Lower End of Beaver Falls. At first a celebrity on campus and later headlined on sports pages everywhere, Joe began to thrive on publicity and public attention. There wasn't very much time left for the classroom; he later switched to an industrial arts major ("manual training," he says) and has yet to graduate.

The Southern fans were the first to call him "Joe Willie" (his middle name is William), but he

JOE WAS STILL WEARING BLACK SHOES WHEN ALABAMA DEFEATED OKLAHOMA IN THE 1963 ORANGE BOWL.

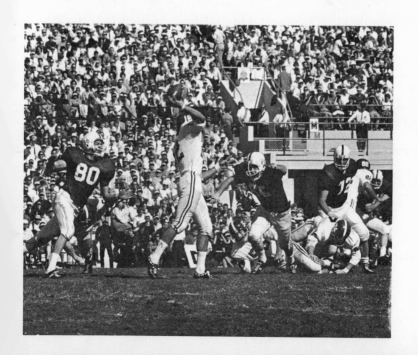

was also known as "Nigger" Namath at Alabama for a time because of his Lower End friends and his dark complexion. Alabama is one of the Southern states where the white population has clung most strongly to racial separation, and Negroes were not even admitted to the University until the summer between Joe's sophomore and junior years. Many students could not understand Joe's ideas of racial equality and argued with him in favor of segregation and white supremacy. Joe was later quoted by the press as having commented, "They were raised a different way than I was, so I didn't try to tell them how to live."

Joe missed the last game of his junior year and also the Sugar Bowl game against Mississippi the following January. He had been suspended from the squad by Coach Bryant for having broken training by staying out too late and going to parties. (So seriously do Alabamans take their football that Bryant had to explain his reasons for the suspension on statewide television.)

Called by Joe the "roughest thing I've had to face," the punishment has been credited with being a turning point in his career. The following season he was a much stronger team player, and his center was quoted as saying, "He was a real leader . . . for the first time."

One reason for Joe's taking his suspension so seriously was his great respect for Bear Bryant. Much of Joe's fiery competitiveness and strong will to win were instilled by Bryant, who bitterly hates to lose. Joe says of him, "I just believe he's not only a great coach but a great man."

During his senior year, Joe suffered the first of his widely discussed knee troubles. As he was rolling out of the pocket on a quarterback-option play (run or pass, depending on how the defense moves) in the North Carolina State game, his right knee suddenly collapsed, and he fell. Joe now thinks the cause was bent cleats on his right shoe, but two weeks later the same thing happened while he was playing against Florida. Then, while practicing for the Orange Bowl against Texas, he injured the knee even more seriously.

The bad knee kept Joe from starting in the Orange Bowl game, but after Texas had gone ahead of Alabama he finally convinced Coach Bryant to let him play. Limping badly, but throwing well, he completed eighteen passes and almost saved the game; but Texas stubbornly persisted. The Longhorns stopped Joe late in the game just inches from their goal line and won 21–17.

The following day Joe signed a three-year contract with the AFL New York Jets for a reported

AS A SENIOR AT ALABAMA, JOE WAS ONE OF THE OUTSTANDING
QUARTERBACKS OF COLLEGIATE FOOTBALL.

$427,000. This contract made him the highest-paid rookie in the history of professional football at the time, and immediately attracted the attention of newspaper, magazine, radio and television sports reporters. They've been following Joe around ever since.

3

ROOKIE JOE

As an All-American quarterback at one of the strongest football colleges in the country, Joe was bound to receive a lot of attention from the pro scouts and recruiters. Unfamiliar with business negotiations—the most money he had ever had at one time until then was six hundred dollars—he appointed an Alabama lawyer to handle the complicated bargaining and maneuvering for him.

During these dealings, some very large sums of money were mentioned. The NFL St. Louis Cardinals are said to have gone as high as $325,000 in the bidding, but the AFL New York Jets went even higher. The amount of Joe's three-year, no-cut contract usually mentioned is $427,000, although that figure probably also included the lawyer's fee, scouting salaries for Joe's brothers and brother-in-law, and the cost of a Lincoln Continental convertible for Joe.

In any case, it was by far the largest salary and bonus ever offered to a rookie at the time, and it indirectly led to the merger of the two leagues. Further competition the following year between the AFL and the NFL for new players drove salaries and bonuses even higher. Two players switched leagues for more money, and several others were rumored to be planning to do so. In financial self-defense, the previously warring leagues wisely decided to merge. When the announcement of the merger was made, Joe was reported to have said, "I got out of college just in time."

The Jets had finished only their second season as a functioning team a few weeks before they signed Joe. The American Football League itself dates only from 1960, and the New York City AFL club between 1960 and 1963 was a rinky-dink outfit misnamed the Titans. While the level of play throughout the AFL during its beginning years generally left something to be desired, that of the Titans was just plain terrible. Very few New Yorkers came out

FLANKED BY COACH WEEB EWBANK (LEFT) AND JET PRESIDENT SONNY WERBLIN, JOE SPEAKS AT A PRESS LUNCHEON SHORTLY AFTER SIGNING WITH THE NEW YORK TEAM.

to watch the Titans' games, the players were seldom paid on time, and before long the team went bankrupt.

In 1963 the club was taken over by a group headed by David "Sonny" Werblin, a highly successful show-business executive with much experience in television. He changed the name of the team to the Jets, hired a topflight coach (Weeb Ewbank, formerly with Baltimore in the NFL), and made preparations to move the Jet games from the tacky Polo Grounds out to beautiful Shea Stadium on Long Island. Most important of all, he began looking for more capable players.

Werblin, who had been influential in the careers of such show-business figures as Frank Sinatra and Jackie Gleason, particularly wanted a colorful superstar who would capture the imagination of New Yorkers, give them something to talk about during the week, and then bring them out to the games on Sundays. Recalling his experience in the entertainment world, he searched for an accomplished athlete with a strong and appealing personality, a true star in the theatrical as well as sports sense. He is convinced that he has found his star in Joe Willie Namath.

"You know how a real star lights up the room when he comes in. Joe has that quality," Werblin once said; and, as he added on another occasion, "Stars sell tickets."

Star or not, Joe's first task as a Jet was to go to the hospital. In January of 1965, Jet team physician

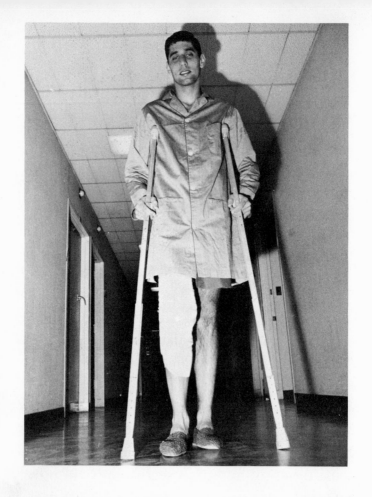

THE FIRST OF TWO OPERATIONS ON JOE'S RIGHT KNEE WAS PERFORMED IN JANUARY, 1965.

and orthopedic surgeon Dr. James Nicholas, who had helped to fuse the spine of President Kennedy, operated on Joe's right knee in an attempt to repair the damage done the previous fall at Alabama. Forty reporters were at the hospital to cover the operation, and their detailed stories plus the continuing discussion about his contract kept the papers full of Joe Willie for some time. Even people who rarely followed football became aware of the Jets, and some commentators said that Werblin had his money's worth from Joe before he ever put on the green and white uniform.

Joe was out of the hospital in two weeks, but he continued to exercise his much-publicized right knee (the best-known joint in America, one joke said) with a forty-pound weight all through the winter, spring and summer. By the time training camp opened in late summer, the knee seemed strong enough, but it was only one of several problems facing Joe.

Stepping up from college ball to the far more demanding pros is never easy, and many highly ranked school stars have failed altogether. In Joe's case it would be all the harder because of his big salary and advance publicity. Could he live up to his notices, and what would be the reaction of the rest of the team?

While some resentment of Joe's money and publicity did exist at first, most of the veterans soon realized that his arrival meant improvement for the team and for the league. Not only that, "I figure it's going to mean more money for the rest of us," one said.

The other players were also impressed by Joe's ability and his attitude. He worked hard, practicing long hours to improve the timing and accuracy of his passes, and he carefully studied the nearly three hundred offensive plays in the Jets' playbook. Accustomed to only two or three defenses in college, he also spent much time familiarizing himself with the dozen defensive arrangements used by the pros. Like most rookie quarterbacks before him, he found his toughest job was learning to "read" the defense for the type of pass coverage it was about to employ.

Most of all, however, it was Joe's good-natured personality that helped to remove any bitterness that remained. As the other Jets got to know him, they found Joe a highly likable young man, and since they already respected his ability, his acceptance was assured. When a general meeting was called to give players a chance to voice gripes and offer suggestions, Joe asked that anyone resenting his salary speak up so that dissension could be avoided before the season started. There were no replies. One old-timer has said, "There were only a few guys putting the zinger to him by then and after he gave them the chance to say what they had to say in public and they didn't, they had to shut up— in public anyway."

There was also the controversy about Joe's draft status to concern him. A few people had complained that if he were healthy enough to be playing a rough sport like football, he should be in the Army instead. But when his draft board called Joe back to Beaver Falls for a physical examination, the doctors rejected him as unfit for military service because of his injured knee.

JOE'S FIRST PRO GAME WAS AN EXHIBITION CONTEST AGAINST BOSTON IN JULY, 1965. HE THREW FOR TWO TOUCHDOWNS AS THE JETS WON, 23–6.

A small amount of public indignation flared for a time, but most reporters thought the Army had applied the same standards of selection to Joe as to everyone else. Joe himself was widely quoted as asking a reporter from *Sports Illustrated,* "How can I win, man? If I say I'm glad, I'm a traitor, and if I say I'm sorry, I'm a fool."

A rookie quarterback seldom gets much playing time in the pros, usually taking about three years to develop. But the 1965 Jets had traded away their first-string quarterback, Dick Wood, and were counting on either Joe, Mike Taliaferro (pronounced "Tolliver"), or John Huarte to take his place. Taliaferro had been a 1964 rookie playing behind Wood, and Huarte, the Notre Dame star, was another first-year man, signed shortly after Joe.

Huarte played in the College All-Star game that summer, missing much of the Jets' training camp; he never really caught up to the others and was later traded to the Boston Patriots. When Weeb Ewbank announced he would choose his quarterback on a game-to-game basis depending on practice performance, his choice was therefore understood to be between Mike and Joe.

Joe didn't get into the first game of the season, a loss to Houston, Mike going all the way.

Joe did play a large part of the Kansas City game the following week, however, and had a fine night, completing eleven passes including one for a touchdown. But the Jets lost to Kansas City, they lost to Buffalo the next week (Joe's first starting game), and they also lost to Denver. It was about this time that a reporter asked Joe what the difference between college and pro ball was, and Joe growled, "Losing!"

Although doing very well for a first-year man, Joe was still learning the complicated job of running the Jets' offense as well as bringing his passing up to professional standards. During the next few games (a tie, another loss, and—finally—two victories), he spent more time on the bench studying the action to correct errors in his play.

By the time of the first Boston game, he had improved enough to play the entire sixty minutes; throwing two touchdown passes, he led the Jets to a 30–20 win over the Patriots. The following week he looked even better, completing four touchdown passes to drub Houston 41–14. The Jets had won four straight, and Joe had become the only rookie starting quarterback in either league.

As the weeks went by, the verdict came in from sports writers and fans alike: Joe Willie really could

JET COACHES, LOCATED HIGH IN SHEA STADIUM FOR A BETTER
OVERALL VIEW, RELAY GAME INFORMATION TO JOE THROUGH A
FIELD TELEPHONE ON THE SIDELINES.

throw as quickly and as accurately as the Jet man-
agement had promised, and he did have a flair and
sparkle that set him apart. There was general agree-
ment that he would soon be one of the biggest stars
in professional football.

When the Jets finished their 1965 schedule by
beating the champion Buffalo Bills, Joe had achieved
a record that would have done credit to an established veteran, not to mention a rookie who had
not played every game. Statistically he ranked as
the league's third best passer, with one hundred

sixty-four completions in three hundred and forty attempts for a 2,220-yard total and a .482 percentage, and eighteen touchdown passes. Voted the American Football League Rookie of the Year by United Press International, he was also the only rookie on the AFL All-Star team.

When the All-Stars played the league-champion Buffalo Bills in January of 1966, Joe gave a par-

DURING THE 1966 AFL ALL-STAR GAME, JOE THREW TWO TOUCH-DOWN PASSES TO SAN DIEGO END LANCE ALWORTH.

ticularly impressive performance. The Stars were behind 13 to 6 at the half, but when Joe came in he sparked them to a 30–19 victory, throwing for two of the touchdowns. He was later named Most Valuable Player of the game.

He slightly strained his right knee again during a 1966 exhibition game, but was able to play throughout the regular season, wearing his usual rubber-padded metal knee brace. His special white low-cut shoes were also wedged inside the heels to allow him greater freedom of movement; and the cleats were shortened so that his feet would leave the ground quickly when he was hit and not stick in the turf to strain his knee further.

During 1966, Joe's right knee became arthritic (inflamed in the joint) and needed to be reduced with ice packs when it swelled and ached after each game. As a result of favoring the right knee, he developed bursitis, a different kind of inflammation, in his left knee and had to wear a second brace to protect it. Joe ran with the ball only as a last resort, and when he did had orders from Coach Ewbank to head for the sidelines and out of bounds to minimize the chance of further injury. Even so, he scored two touchdowns against Oakland by running.

LEAPING HIGH IN THE AIR, JOE THROWS ONE OF HIS FIVE TOUCHDOWN PASSES AGAINST THE HOUSTON OILERS ON SEPTEMBER 18, 1966.

Despite his painful handicap, Joe got the Jets off to a fast start on the 1966 season, beating Miami, Houston and Denver on successive Sundays. The Houston game was the home opener, and when Joe threw five touchdown passes the fans at Shea Stadium were ecstatic. In their fourth game, the Jets tied Boston with a stirring fourth-quarter seventeen-point rally, highlighted by Joe's completion of fourteen of twenty-three passes for two hundred and five yards and two touchdowns. When they next squeaked past rugged San Diego by a single point, the Jets led the Eastern Division. But then a poor running game and the loss of several starting players through injuries caught up with them, and they dropped their next four games. They went on to win one, tie one, and lose two more before upsetting Boston in their last game to salvage a .500 season.

In 1966, his first full year as a number-one quarterback, Joe's passing was fourth best in the league. He completed two hundred thirty-two passes of four hundred seventy-one attempts for a .493 average and a total of 3,379 yards. He threw touchdown passes nineteen times during the season and brought the Jets to a third-place finish in the East behind Buffalo and Boston.

Not only had the Jets become a good ball club, they were also making money. In 1966 they outdrew every other team in the league by well over 100,000 fans, an enormous improvement over the days of the bumbling Titans. The future seemed bright indeed for Werblin, Ewbank, Namath and company, and a championship team was very much in their plans

before many more seasons went by.

4

BROADWAY JOE

NEW YORKERS have always admired sports figures, and New York professional teams of the past have boasted such famous stars as Babe Ruth, Joe DiMaggio, Jackie Robinson, Willie Mays and Y. A. Tittle. But the Dodgers and baseball Giants moved from New York some time ago, and during the middle sixties the formerly great Yankees and football Giants declined to last-place teams and began a period of rebuilding. Yogi Berra had retired, Mickey Mantle was nearing the end of his playing career, scrambling Fran Tarkenton had not yet been imported by the Giants, and New York fans were gradually being left without a superstar to cheer at the stadium and follow in their sports pages at home.

Until Joe Namath came to town, that is. His fast eye at spotting receivers combined with his rapid-fire delivery of the football immediately excited the spectators, and his likable personality, good looks and lively off-field activities made good copy for the highly active New York press. Soon everyone was talking about Joe, and one AFL owner was reported to have called him "the biggest thing in New York since Babe Ruth."

A wave of articles about Joe appeared in national magazines, and he was soon in demand as a guest star on network television programs which featured celebrities of interest to the general public. Even people with little knowledge of football became interested in Joe Willie's career, and not only New York, but the entire sports world had a new superstar.

Joe quickly became known as a Broadway personality as well as a sports notable and appeared in one of his magazine-cover photographs wearing his Jets uniform in the middle of Times Square. Single ("I'd rather go to Vietnam than get married"), the sociable athlete spends much of his free time lounging about the discotheques and clubs of Manhattan with people in show business. "He likes

BROADWAY JOE TRIES HIS DARK GLASSES ON BARBRA STREISAND'S
POODLE BACKSTAGE AT THE WINTERGARDEN THEATER.

the lights," says Sonny Werblin, in a considerable understatement.

Joe once defended his flashy night life by saying, "I believe in letting a guy live the way he wants to if he doesn't hurt anyone." He has also carried that point of view over to his apartment on the upper East Side of Manhattan. The apartment, which he shares with a Jet teammate he first knew at Alabama and a writer for a horseracing newspaper, has a marble floor, silk wallpaper and gold-plated bathroom fixtures. Even more unusual is its truly fantastic wall-to-wall white llama rug, six inches thick and reported to have cost $10,000.

In spite of these gaudy trappings, most people have found Joe to be essentially friendly, modest and very likable. Six feet two and a hundred and ninety-five pounds with a slouching walk, he has a shock of black hair usually cut much longer than most professional athletes, high cheekbones, and a quick wide grin. He still has a fondness for pizza between meals, and he jokes frequently, often at his own expense, in speech that has been softened by the four years in Alabama.

While not anxious to return to Beaver Falls, Joe maintains his family ties and dutifully shaved off a beard and mustache he once grew because his

EVEN WHEN HE IS NOT PLAYING, JOE ATTRACTS ATTENTION. HE
WORE THIS UNUSUAL COSTUME ON THE SIDELINES AFTER BEING
INJURED IN AN EXHIBITION GAME.

mother complained he did not look like a Hungarian. He has arranged Jets' scouting jobs for two of his brothers and his sister's husband, and the brothers also manage an insurance agency which Joe has set up.

There are some who say that worry over a brother's health was the primary reason for Joe's mysterious disappearance from training camp just before the first exhibition game of the 1967 season. He was later accused of having been involved in a night-club scuffle in New York, but Joe denied the charge. Although the incident attracted much unfavorable publicity, Joe's teammates accepted his explanation of concern over personal problems and continue to respect him as their leader.

However, it is for his performance on the field that Joe must first be judged, and there is also controversy there. In 1967 he ranked as the third best passer in the AFL, completing 258 passes for a total of 4,007 yards and setting a record for one season's passing yardage in both the AFL and NFL. But Joe also led the AFL in passes intercepted in 1966 and 1967, although his fans do point out that he has thrown more often than the other quarterbacks because of the Jets' weak running game.

This unevenness in Joe's play was a striking

JOE WRIGGLED AWAY FROM THIS BUFFALO TACKLE, BUT THE PASS THAT FOLLOWED WAS INTERCEPTED.

feature of the 1968 AFL East-West All-Star game. After being intercepted three times during the first half, he rallied in the second half and threw a touchdown pass with six minutes to go. Then—with only fifty-eight seconds left—he scored from the one-yard line himself and gave the East an upset 25–24 victory over the West.

Joe will be working hard in the future to reduce his interception percentage and to refine his play calling, but his running will necessarily be limited. And, of course, there will always be the question of the durability of his knees as long as he plays.

The right knee was operated upon again at the end of the 1966 season, and again there was a vast amount of publicity. At training camp the next summer Joe was first quoted as saying, "I'm just not sure about this rascal," but after a few days working out he was able to move about much more easily than before and boasted, "It hasn't felt better in years."

During 1967 Joe was a more flexible quarterback, even rolling out of the pocket and running occasionally when his receivers were covered. His increased mobility and experience combined with an improved defense to give the Jets their most successful year since the creation of the team. Two familiar problems—injuries to key running backs and a losing streak in the second half of the season —held them to a second-place finish in the Eastern

JOE'S FANS ARE CONVINCED THAT HE WILL BECOME THE BEST QUARTERBACK IN FOOTBALL.

Division, but they were the only team to beat league champion Oakland during the regular season.

Joe's cheekbone was broken during the next-to-last game of the 1967 schedule, a defeat by Oakland. Ben Davidson, the defensive end who tackled him, later quoted Joe as saying, "I've been beat up worse by girls." By the last game of the season, against San Diego, the Jets had been eliminated from the divisional championship, but Joe wore a protective mask and played the entire afternoon. He threw four touchdown passes to end the season with a victory.

In March of 1968, Joe returned to the hospital for his third knee operation. This time it was to correct the bursitis condition in his left knee. If the doctors can keep his knees functioning and he continues to improve at his present rate, he is very likely to be the leading quarterback of both leagues within a few seasons. And, because he has become an established star at a much earlier age than those who preceded him, he could eventually develop into one of the greatest passers of all time. Weeb Ewbank, who once coached no less a passer than Johnny Unitas, calls Joe the best prospect since Sammy Baugh, the famous Washington Redskin quarterback generally regarded as one of the best passers in the history of football.

Whatever lies ahead for Joe Willie Namath, he has already become a genuine superstar at an age when most other young men are just getting started in their first real jobs. The opportunities for Joe to further prove himself seem great, and his thousands of fans are certain that he can measure up to the challenge.